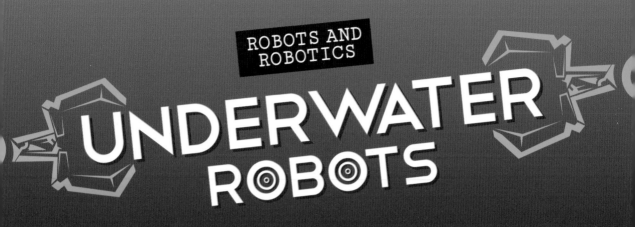

ROBOTS AND ROBOTICS

UNDERWATER ROBOTS

DANIEL R. FAUST

PowerKiDS press

New York

Published in 2017 by The Rosen Publishing Group, Inc.
29 East 21st Street, New York, NY 10010

First Edition

Editor: Caitie McAneney
Book Design: Reann Nye

Photo Credits: Cover Luis Lamar/National Geographic/Getty Images; p. 4 STAN HONDA/AFP/Getty Images; p. 5 Patrick Aventurier/Getty Images News/Getty Images; p. 6 https://commons.wikimedia.org/wiki/File:REMUS_100_Merivoimien_vuosip%C3%A4iv%C3%A4_2014_01.JPG; p. 7 AFP/Pool/Getty Images; p. 8 https://commons.wikimedia.org/wiki/File:Cutletrov.jpg; p. 10 https://en.wikipedia.org/wiki/File:Seaexplorer_diving.jpg; p. 11 https://commons.wikimedia.org/wiki/Category:Sonar#/media/File:Collecting_Multibeam_Sonar_Data.jpg; p. 14 Matt9122/Shutterstock.com; p. 15 https://commons.wikimedia.org/wiki/File:RoboTuna,_1994,_view_2_-_MIT_Museum_-_DSC03730.JPG; p. 17 (AUV) https://en.wikipedia.org/wiki/File:BPAUV-MP_from_HSV-.jpg; p. 17 (ROV) https://commons.wikimedia.org/wiki/File:ROV_Hercules_2005.JPG; p. 17 (HOV) xavier gallego morell/Shutterstock.com; p. 18 Ralph White/Getty Images; p. 19 TANNEN MAURY/AFP/Getty Images; p. 21 EVARISTO SA/AFP/Getty Images; p. 22 Navin Mistry/Shutterstock.com; p. 23 https://commons.wikimedia.org/wiki/File:SEALAB_II.jpg; p. 24 https://commons.wikimedia.org/wiki/File:Mine_neutralization_vehicle_MNV.jpg; p. 25 https://en.wikipedia.org/wiki/File:US_Navy_060612-N-4124C-065_Mineman_3rd_Class_Dustin_Moore,_assigned_to_the_mine_warfare_ship_USS_Patriot; p. 26 J Pat Carter/ASSOCIATED PRESS/AP Images; p. 27 Alexander Davidyuk/Shuttersrtock.com; p. 29 Michael Karas/ASSOCIATED PRESS/AP Images; p. 30 Iakov Filimonov/Shutterstock.com.

Library of Congress Cataloging-in-Publication Data

Names: Faust, Daniel R.
Title: Underwater robots / Daniel R. Faust.
Description: New York : PowerKids Press, [2016] | Series: Robots and robotics | Includes index.
Identifiers: LCCN 2016012340 | ISBN 9781499421866 (pbk.) | ISBN 9781499421880 (library bound) | ISBN 9781499421873 (6 pack)
Subjects: LCSH: Remote submersibles–Juvenile literature. | Robots–Juvenile literature.
Classification: LCC TC1662 .F38 2016 | DDC 623.82/7-dc23
LC record available at http://lccn.loc.gov/2016012340

Manufactured in the United States of America

CPSIA Compliance Information: Batch #BS16PK: For Further Information contact Rosen Publishing, New York, New York at 1-800-237-9932

CONTENTS

DANGERS OF THE DEEP

Is it possible to explore every inch of Earth's surface? Exploring the land might be possible, but oceans cover almost three-quarters of our planet. Scientists have divided the ocean into five layers, or zones. Each zone is darker and colder than the one above it. In addition to the darkness and low temperatures, the pressure of the deep ocean is enough to crush an unprotected person. That makes ocean exploration very dangerous, or unsafe.

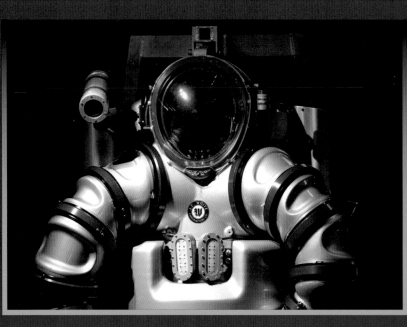

In order to work deep underwater for long periods of time, people need to wear special suits. These bulky suits provide oxygen and protection from extreme pressure and freezing temperatures.

In order to explore and work deep underwater, some people rely on special underwater robots. These robots can be preprogrammed to operate **autonomously** or a human pilot can operate them remotely. Underwater robots allow us to explore shipwrecks, discover new sea life, study ocean currents, and much more.

AUV OR ROV?

Underwater robots are known as unmanned underwater vehicles, or UUVs. These are similar to unmanned **aerial** vehicles (UAV), or drones. That's why UUVs are sometimes called underwater drones. Like UAVs, UUVs are vehicles designed to operate without a human operator onboard.

MEET REMUS

REMUS robots, or Remote Environmental Monitoring UnitS, are a kind of inexpensive AUV. These **torpedo**-shaped robots are used for surveying and mapping the ocean. They're controlled by a simple laptop computer and driven by a propeller and fins. Using **sonar** and other sensors, the robot's onboard computer gathers and records data about the ocean environment. There are several different REMUS models available. Each one is suitable for different tasks, including deep-sea exploration and underwater tunnel inspection. The U.S. Navy has even used REMUS robots to detect underwater **mines**.

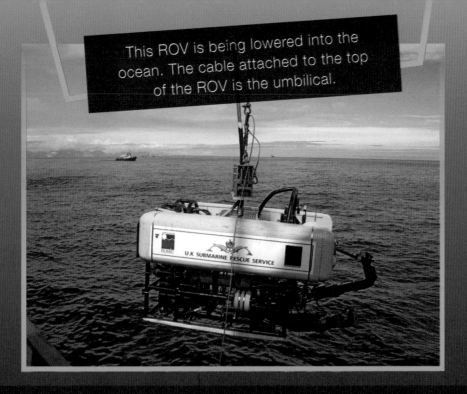

This ROV is being lowered into the ocean. The cable attached to the top of the ROV is the umbilical.

There are two different kinds of unmanned underwater vehicles. The first is called a remotely operated vehicle, or ROV. ROVs require an operator to direct them from a distance. ROVs are controlled and powered through an umbilical. An umbilical is a cable or series of cables that connects the ROV to a ship. It sends commands from the operator to the ROV.

Autonomous underwater vehicles, or AUVs, operate without direct input from an operator. They're preprogrammed with commands. AUVs can dive much deeper than ROVs.

FIRST UNDERWATER ROBOTS

During World War I and World War II, pilots used aerial torpedoes against enemy ships and submarines. An aerial torpedo is a self-propelled missile that is dropped into the water from an airplane or helicopter. The torpedo travels underwater until it reaches its target.

The earliest UUVs were developed in the years after World War II. At that time, navies around the world began to develop remotely operated underwater vehicles. The Cutlet was an unmanned **submersible** used by Britain's Royal Navy beginning in the 1950s. Its job was to recover practice mines and torpedoes. In the 1960s, the U.S. Navy developed the Cable-Controlled Underwater Recovery Vehicle, or CURV, to perform deep-sea rescues and recover objects from the ocean floor.

The Royal Navy's Cutlet was one of the first ROVs. You can see the simple claw it used to grasp torpedoes and mines.

TIMELINE OF UNDERWATER ROBOTS

1864
The first programmed underwater vehicle (PUV), a torpedo, is developed in Austria.

1914
The first aerial torpedo is dropped during World War I.

1950s
Cutlet is developed by the British Royal Navy to recover practice torpedoes.

1957
The first AUV, named SPURV (Special Purpose Underwater Research Vehicle), is developed at the University of Washington.

1960s
The U.S. Navy funds early ROV technology development for rescue and recovery operations.

1974
RCV-225 becomes one of the first commercial ROVs to be developed.

1988
Jason and Medea, a two-body ROV system, is launched by the Woods Hole Oceanographic Institution.

1995
The Autonomous Benthic Explorer (ABE) becomes the first AUV of its kind. It's able to move on its own for long periods of time.

2009
Nereus, a half-ROV and half-AUV, reaches the deepest part of the ocean—the Mariana Trench.

HOW DO ROBOTS WORK?

Like other robots, unmanned underwater robots come in many different shapes and sizes. Many are built in the shape of traditional torpedoes with a thin body and pointed nose. Some UUVs have a modular design, which means they have components, or parts, that can be removed and replaced depending on the robot's job. All underwater robots require sensors, navigation equipment, **propulsion**, and a power source.

SEAEXPLORER UUV

We rely on sonar to detect what's under the surface of the ocean. Sonar can tell the size, shape, and distance of objects under the water. This shows what a multibeam sonar system looks like. It uses multiple beams to collect more data.

The sensors used on underwater robots are a little different than those found on other robots. With little or no sunlight, video cameras don't always work in deep water. Some underwater robots have powerful lights so their cameras can work. Others rely on special sensors that detect magnetic fields, temperature, or electrical currents. Most underwater robots are equipped with compasses, depth sensors, and sonar equipment.

Underwater navigation can be difficult and problematic. Radio waves don't travel far underwater, so most UUVs can't use **GPS**. AUVs need to use their other sensors to navigate. An AUV figures out where it is based on its last known position and how fast and far it's traveled from that point.

The most common device for propulsion in underwater robots is a propeller, like the kind used on boats and ships of all sizes. There are also UUVs called underwater gliders that don't propel themselves directly. Gliders repeatedly sink and rise, transforming this up-and-down motion into forward movement. The propellers and other equipment need power to work. Rechargeable batteries power most underwater robots.

THE FOUR PARTS OF A ROBOT

Whether they're built to operate on land, in the air, or underwater, all robots have the same four basic parts. Effectors are the parts of the robot that interact with the environment. Actuators are the motors that move the robot's other parts, including its arms, wheels, or propellers. Sensors act like the robot's eyes and ears, gathering information about the robot's surroundings. Everything works thanks to the controller, which is the onboard computer that acts like the robot's brain.

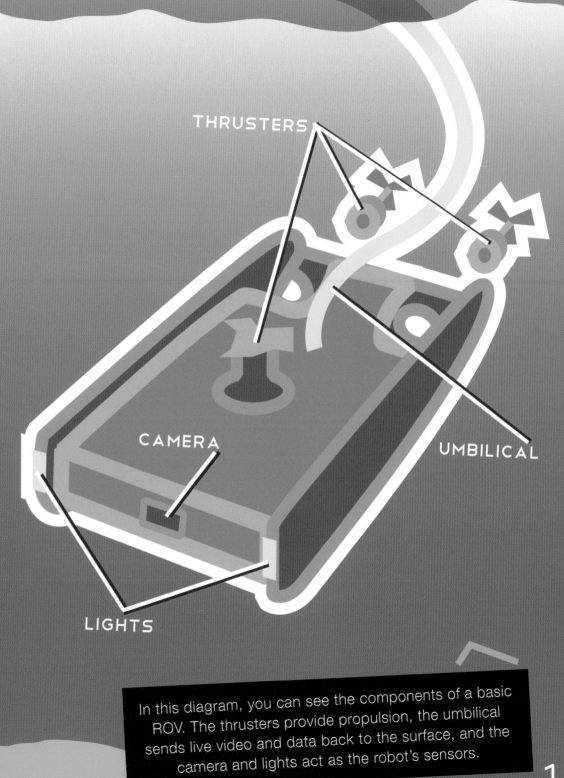

THRUSTERS

UMBILICAL

CAMERA

LIGHTS

In this diagram, you can see the components of a basic ROV. The thrusters provide propulsion, the umbilical sends live video and data back to the surface, and the camera and lights act as the robot's sensors.

LEARNING FROM NATURE

In order to build better robots, engineers are looking to the natural world. Biomimicry is a method of solving engineering problems by studying things in nature and **mimicking** them. Engineers study birds and insects to design more efficient flying robots. Engineers also study fish and other sea life, trying to copy how they move in water to build a better underwater robot.

Scientists at the Massachusetts Institute of Technology (MIT) built the RoboTuna in 1994. It was one of the first attempts to build a robot that could move the way a fish moves.

Scientists and engineers are designing new underwater robots with flexible body parts that will allow the robots to move through the water the way a fish does. Other designs mimic the gliding motion of manta rays. Another design is an eight-legged robot based on a lobster. It's designed to move along the bottom of rivers, lakes, and other bodies of water that aren't too deep.

15

UNDERWATER EXPLORATION

About 71 percent of the Earth's surface is covered by water. However, nearly 95 percent of the underwater world hasn't been explored yet. Many scientists are working to continue ocean exploration and learn more about the deep sea. From special diving suits to submersible vehicles, explorers and scientists have developed many tools and techniques to safely explore the ocean depths.

Robots are used as replacements for humans in many dangerous situations, from military operations to space exploration. Underwater exploration is just another dangerous situation where robots are used in place of people. Underwater robots don't need to breathe and they can survive the extreme pressure and low temperatures of the deep sea. Their sensors are also capable of detecting things in the darkness that human eyes would never be able to see.

Scientists and explorers use different kinds of vehicles to study the ocean depths. What's the difference between AUVs, ROVs, and HOVs?

DIVE AND EXPLORE!

AUV

name means: autonomous underwater vehicle
special parts: thrusters, batteries, navigation, onboard computer, manipulator arm, camera, sample basket

ROV

name means: remotely operated vehicle
special parts: thrusters, navigation, umbilical, manipulator arm, onboard computer, camera, sample basket

HOV (SUBMARINE)

name means: human-occupied vehicle
special parts: thrusters, navigation, onboard computer, sample basket, manipulator arm, camera, onboard pilot

The military has used underwater robots to recover objects for many years. **Civilian** organizations use UUVs for similar tasks. Underwater robots are used for locating shipwrecks or airplanes that have crashed in the ocean. These robots have located many historic shipwrecks, including the *Titanic* and the *Bismarck*.

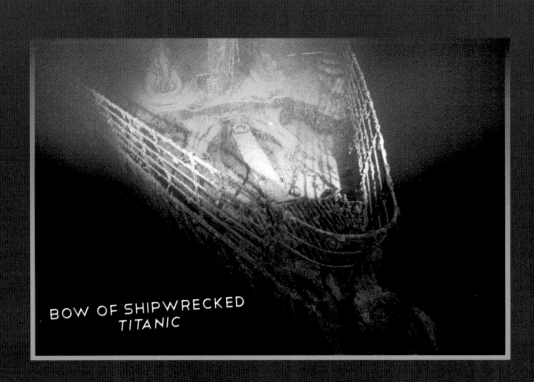
BOW OF SHIPWRECKED TITANIC

Objects, such as this china, were recovered from the wreck of the *Titanic* using remotely operated underwater vehicles.

In the case of the *Titanic*, underwater robots helped recover items that had been on board the ship when it sank. This illustrated that underwater robots would be able to play a key role in the area of underwater **archaeology**. Robots can be used to map **excavation** sites that couldn't be reached by normal means. Smaller, more **maneuverable** robots can closely examine the site and retrieve artifacts, or historical objects.

UNDERWATER ROBOTS AND SCIENCE

Underwater robots have opened up a whole new world of scientific research. Robots have helped scientists discover and identify a number of new plants and animals. They've also allowed scientists to study these plants and animals in their natural environment. Today, UUVs are used to gather data about ocean currents, temperature, and sea life in order to study the effects of climate change.

A number of private and public organizations have used robots to explore the oceans. The Monterey Bay Aquarium Research Institute used the Tiburon robot for deep-sea exploration from 1997 to 2008. The Woods Hole Oceanographic Institute also created an ROV team— the Jason and Medea system—for seafloor exploration. The Canadian Scientific Submersible Facility developed the ROPOS (Remotely Operated Platform for Ocean Sciences) robot, which can explore ocean vents and fix ocean observatories.

UUVs designed for underwater scientific study are often equipped with robotic arms, as well as a special container to hold tools and samples.

CONSTRUCTION AND INSPECTION

In order to live and work underwater, humans need to build special habitats. They're often underwater laboratories where scientists make observations about the ocean environment. These habitats protect scientists from the extreme pressure and temperature of the deep sea. Today, underwater robots can be used to build, maintain, and repair these structures safely and quickly.

This is SEALAB II, which was lowered to the seafloor in 1965. It could house 10 people for 30 days.

Oil and natural gas companies use underwater robots to dig wells and build pipelines in water that's too deep for human workers. They can install and fix underwater cables that provide Internet and phone services to people on shore. Robots are also used to inspect underwater pipelines, making sure that the oil and gas they carry don't pollute the underwater environment. Underwater robots can even be used to inspect what cargo ships are carrying.

UNDERWATER MILITARY ROBOTS

One of the first military tasks for underwater robots was to locate and disarm mines. Although UUVs still perform this task, the military has expanded the role of underwater robots over the years. Underwater robots are effective because they don't require food, oxygen, or rest. They can also be used in dangerous environments, potentially saving the life of a human soldier.

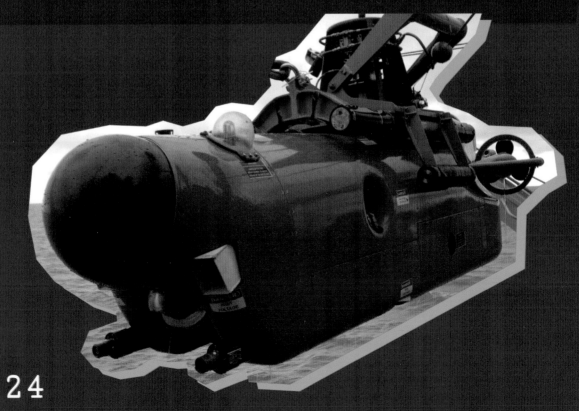

The military uses ROVs, such as this orange mine neutralization vehicle, to detect and remove underwater mines.

Like unmanned ground vehicles and unmanned aerial vehicles, the military uses unmanned underwater vehicles for **surveillance** and **reconnaissance**. The Echo Voyager is an unmanned submarine that can roam the seas on reconnaissance missions for six months at a time. Robots can be used to patrol enemy waters or guard local ports and harbors. Underwater robots can also be used to carry and deliver equipment and inspect ships and submarines. Police departments sometimes use UUVs to aid in search-and-rescue or recovery operations.

Have you ever seen people flying drones in a park or on a playground? Flying these unmanned aerial vehicles has become a popular hobby. Operating UUVs can be a fun hobby, too. There are many models of underwater drones that you can buy, just like flying drones, but many people prefer to build their own drones. Most hobby UUVs can only be operated in the calm waters of lakes or swimming pools.

Because underwater robots can be equipped with cameras, they're becoming increasingly popular with Hollywood and documentary filmmakers. Modern UUVs are cheap, maneuverable, and easy to operate. That makes them useful tools for filming underwater, especially in spaces that are too small for a human diver to reach.

BUILD YOUR OWN

You can easily buy an underwater drone online or at your local hobby shop, but if you're interested in engineering, you might want to build your own. Most homemade underwater robots are built using PVC piping, or the white pipes used in many plumbing systems. You can add lights, cameras, or other sensors to your homemade robots as well.

Once you've built and tested your underwater robot, you might want to enter it in a competition. Marine Advanced Technology Education (MATE) Center is a team of organizations that host a popular underwater robotics competition. Schools and other organizations compete against each other, building their own robots and using them to perform a series of tasks. There may be similar competitions at schools or clubs in your hometown.

With the right parts, it's surprisingly easy to build your own underwater robot.

THE OCEANS OF TOMORROW

The ocean is like an alien environment right here on Earth. Although we have found ways to safely explore the ocean, it's still a dangerous and extreme place. That's one of the benefits of underwater robots. Unmanned underwater vehicles have allowed us to explore the mysteries of the world's oceans.

One day, the ocean may be filled with robots that look just like sea life. Robots built to mimic fish, eels, and lobsters may explore the wonders of the ocean floor. These efficient, maneuverable machines may be able to explore previously unknown regions of the ocean. The military is even experimenting with underwater combat drones similar to the weaponized UAVs and UGVs already in use. As technology advances, who knows what kinds of robots will work in tomorrow's oceans?

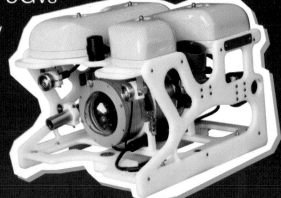

GLOSSARY

aerial: Occurring in the air.

archaeology: The study of past human life based on what those people left behind.

autonomous: Not controlled by others or outside forces.

civilian: A nonmilitary person.

excavation: The process of uncovering something by removing the earth around it.

GPS: A navigating system that uses satellite signals to tell the user where they are and direct them to a destination.

maneuverable: Able to change position easily.

mimic: To copy the way something looks, acts, or sounds.

mine: An explosive often buried in the ground or hidden underwater.

propulsion: The force that moves something forward.

reconnaissance: The exploration of a place to collect information.

sonar: A machine that uses sound waves to find things in a body of water.

submersible: A device designed for underwater work or exploration.

surveillance: The act of watching someone or something closely.

torpedo: A rocket-shaped exploding device that travels underwater.

INDEX

WEBSITES

Due to the changing nature of Internet links, PowerKids Press has developed an
online list of websites related to the subject of this book. This site is updated regularly.
Please use this link to access the list: www.powerkidslinks.com/rar/water